GAIL DEVERS

OVERCOMING ADVERSITY

GAIL DEVERS

Richard Worth

Introduction by James Scott Brady,
Trustee, the Center to Prevent Handgun Violence
Vice Chairman, the Brain Injury Foundation

Chelsea House Publishers
Philadelphia

CHELSEA HOUSE PUBLISHERS

EDITOR IN CHIEF Sally Cheney
DIRECTOR OF PRODUCTION Kim Shinners
PRODUCTION MANAGER Pamela Loos
ART DIRECTOR Sara Davis

SENIOR EDITOR John Ziff
PRODUCTION EDITOR Diann Grasse
LAYOUT 21st Century Publishing and Communications, Inc.

First Printing

1 3 5 7 9 8 6 4 2

The Chelsea House World Wide Web address is
http://www.chelseahouse.com

Library of Congress Cataloging-in-Publication Data

Worth, Richard.
    Gail Devers / Richard Worth.
        p. cm. — (Overcoming adversity)
    Includes bibliographical references and index.
    Contents: "I knew I was back!"—Beginning to race—Graves' Disease—Women
and the Olympic Games—Mind and body—On to Atlanta—Gail keeps on running.
    ISBN 0-7910-6305-4 (alk. paper)
     1. Devers, Gail, 1966- 2. Runners—United States—Biography—Juvenile
literature. [1. Devers, Gail, 1966- 2. Runners (Sports) 3. Women—Biography.
4. African Americans—Biography.] I. Title. II. Series.

GV1061.15.D49 W67 2001
796.42'2'092—dc21
[B]
                                                                2001047597

CONTENTS

OVERCOMING ADVERSITY

TIM ALLEN
comedian/performer

MAYA ANGELOU
author

APOLLO 13 MISSION
astronauts

LANCE ARMSTRONG
professional cyclist

DREW BARRYMORE
actress

DREW CAREY
comedian/performer

JIM CARREY
comedian/performer

BILL CLINTON
U.S. president

TOM CRUISE
actor

GAIL DEVERS
Olympian

MICHAEL J. FOX
actor

MOHANDAS K. GANDHI
political/spiritual leader

WHOOPI GOLDBERG
comedian/performer

EKATERINA GORDEEVA
figure skater

SCOTT HAMILTON
figure skater

JEWEL
singer and poet

JAMES EARL JONES
actor

QUINCY JONES
musician and producer

MARIO LEMIEUX
hockey legend

ABRAHAM LINCOLN
U.S. president

JOHN McCAIN
political leader

WILLIAM PENN
Pennsylvania's founder

JACKIE ROBINSON
baseball legend

ROSEANNE
entertainer

MONICA SELES
tennis star

SAMMY SOSA
baseball star

DAVE THOMAS
entrepreneur

SHANIA TWAIN
entertainer

ROBIN WILLIAMS
performer

BRUCE WILLIS
actor

STEVIE WONDER
entertainer

TRIUMPH OF
THE IMAGINATION:
*The story of writer
J. K. Rowling*

ON FACING ADVERSITY

James Scott Brady

I GUESS IT'S a long way from a Centralia, Illinois, train yard to the George Washington University Hospital Trauma Unit. My dad was a yardmaster for the old Chicago, Burlington & Quincy Railroad. As a child, I used to get to sit in the engineer's lap and imagine what it was like to drive that train. I guess I always have liked being in the "driver's seat."

Years later, however, my interest turned from driving trains to driving campaigns. In 1979, former Texas governor John Connally hired me as a press secretary in his campaign for the American presidency. We lost the Republican primary to a former Hollywood star named Ronald Reagan. But I managed to jump over to the Reagan campaign. When Reagan was elected in 1980, I was "sitting in the catbird seat," as humorist James Thurber would say—poised to be named presidential press secretary. I held that title throughout the eight years of the Reagan administration. But not without one terrible, extended interruption.

It happened barely two months after the Reagan administration took office. I never even heard the shots. On March 30, 1981, my life went blank in an instant. In an attempt to assassinate President Reagan, John Hinckley Jr. armed himself with a "Saturday night special"—a low-quality, $29 pistol—and shot wildly as our presidential entourage exited a Washington hotel. One of the exploding bullets struck me just above the left eye. It shattered into a couple dozen fragments, some of which penetrated my skull and entered my brain.

The next few months of my life were a nightmare of repeated surgery, broken contact with the outside world, and a variety of medical complications. More than once, I was very close to death.

The next few years were filled with frustrating struggles to function with a paralyzed right side, struggles to speak and communicate.

To people who face and defeat daunting obstacles, "ambition" is not becoming wealthy or famous or winning elections or awards. Words like "ambition" and "achievement" and "success" take on very different meanings. The objective is just to live, to wake up every morning. The goals are not lofty; they are very ordinary.

My own heroes are ordinary folks—but they accomplish extraordinary things because they try. My greatest hero is my wife, Sarah. She's accomplished a lot of things in life, but two stand out. The first has been the way she has cared for me and our son since I was shot. A tremendous tragedy and burden was dropped unexpectedly into her life, totally beyond her control and without justification. She could have given up; instead, she focused her energies on preserving our family and returning our lives to normal as much as possible. Week by week, month by month, year by year, she has not reached for the miraculous, just for the normal. Yet in focusing on the normal, she has helped accomplish the miraculous.

Her other most remarkable accomplishment, to me, has been spearheading the effort to keep guns out of the hands of criminals and children in America. Opponents call her a "gun grabber"; I call her a national hero. And I am not alone.

After a seven-year battle, during which Sarah and I worked tirelessly to educate the public about the need for stronger gun laws, the Brady Bill became law in 1993. It was a victory, achieved in the face of tremendous opposition, that now benefits all Americans. From the time the law took effect through fall 1997, background checks had stopped 173,000 criminals and other high-risk purchasers from buying handguns, and the law has helped to reduce illegal gun trafficking.

Sarah was not pursuing fame, or even recognition. She simply started at one point—when our son, Scott, found a loaded handgun on the seat of a pickup truck and, thinking it was a toy, pointed it at Sarah.

Fortunately, no one was hurt. But seeing a gun nearly bring a second tragedy upon our family, Sarah became determined to do whatever she could to prevent senseless death and injury from guns.

Some people think of Sarah as a powerful political force. To me, she's the person who so many times fed me and helped me dress during my long years of recovery.

Overcoming obstacles is part of life, not just for people who are challenged by disabilities, illnesses, or tragedies, but for all people. No matter what the obstacle—fear, disability, prejudice, grief, or a difficulty that isn't likely to "just go away"—we can all work to make this world a better place.

Gail Devers shows off her gold medal after winning the women's 100-meter sprint at the Summer Olympics in Barcelona, Spain, August 1, 1992. The victory was especially remarkable because the previous year she could barely walk, and doctors had considered amputating her feet.

1

"1 KNEW
1 WAS BACK!"

THE XXV SUMMER Olympics opened on July 25, 1992, at a magnificent stadium in Barcelona, Spain. The Olympic torch was lighted with an arrow shot by archer Antonio Rebollo. The opening ceremonies, hosted by King Juan Carlos of Spain, included a colorful reenactment of the birth of the city of Barcelona from the Mediterranean Sea, mock ocean battles featuring colorful sea monsters, and special performances by Spanish opera stars Placido Domingo and José Carreras. In all, 9,367 athletes from 169 countries attended the Summer Games in Barcelona, which featured such great sports stars as basketball's Karl Malone, sprinter and long jumper Carl Lewis, and heptathlon champion Jackie Joyner-Kersee.

For one young American track star, however, these Summer Games were especially poignant. Only 17 months earlier she had been totally unable to set foot on a track. Indeed, doctors had considered amputating her feet, which had swelled, blistered, cracked, and bled, causing her excruciating pain. For Gail Devers, these were the agonizing symptoms of a terrible illness called Graves' disease—a malfunctioning of the thyroid gland. The disease had forced her out of the 1988 Summer Olympics, threatening to bring a complete end to her career. "Deep down I was scared to death that my life as an athlete was over," she said.

But Gail fought back. She was determined not to let the disease defeat her. Eventually, her doctors would figure out how to bring the illness under control with medication, and Gail would begin training again. "I wasn't going to give up," she said. "The word *quit* has never been part of my vocabulary."

Her coach, Bobby Kersee, put Gail on a new training schedule, aimed at preparing her for the 1992 Summer Olympics. Kersee always believed Gail had the potential to be an Olympic star. And he was in a position to know—he had coached Florence Griffith Joyner to three gold medals in track and field in 1988. Gail and Kersee had worked together to prepare her for the 1988 games in Seoul, South Korea, only to see her dream shattered by poor health. Now they began working again.

At first Gail could only walk around a track wearing socks, because her body had so little strength and her feet still hurt. Gradually, she began to jog and finally to sprint. In 1991 at the USA/Mobil Championships—one of the world's most prestigious track and field events—she won the 100-meter hurdles in a time of 12.83 seconds. This was Gail's premier event, the race where she hoped to receive a gold medal at the Olympics. To win she had to jump over a series of hurdles—wooden bars supported by metal stands. It took speed and stamina; one miss and a runner might tumble onto the ground and lose the race. But Gail was up to the challenge. Later in the year she

won another 100-meter hurdle event, this time in Berlin, Germany, setting a new American record at 12.48 seconds. She was the number-one hurdler in the United States.

Gail was now ready to enter the 1992 Olympics. In addition to the hurdles, she would also be competing in the 100-meter sprint. This was another event in which Gail had excelled before the onset of her disease. In the

Barcelona's Olympic stadium, the site of Gail's triumph in the 100 meters at the 1992 Summer Games, lies in the background of this aerial photo. In the foreground is the Catalan National Palace.

Olympic trials, a warm-up for the Games themselves, Gail won the 100-meter hurdles and finished second in the 100-meter sprint. Athletes have to do well in the trials before they are selected to join the U.S. Olympic team.

Finally, she entered the Olympics in Barcelona, ready to win. But there was a problem. The thyroid disease, which had seemed under control, started to act up again. At the U.S. Olympic semifinals—the qualifying heats for the final race—Gail began having muscle spasms. "It's starting all over again," she thought, as she began to feel numbness in her feet when she stood in the starting blocks. "Bobby! I can't feel my leg," she told Coach Kersee after the race was over.

But Gail didn't quit. On Saturday evening, August 1, 1992, Gail was in the starting blocks again, ready to run the race of her life. When the starting gun sounded, Gail got a tremendous start. She was running ahead of her strongest challengers—Jamaica's Juliet Cuthbert, Irina Privalova of the Commonwealth of Independent States (the former Soviet Union), Gwen Torrence of the United States, and Merlene Ottey of Jamaica. But as the race continued, these four challengers began to move on Gail relentlessly, until all five women seemed to be running neck and neck. As they neared the finish line, it looked like anybody's race to win. Would it be Gail or one of her opponents? As they reached the finish, Gail stuck her head forward and seemed to cross just ahead of everyone else.

But the judges weren't so sure. They looked at the replays, and at last decided that Gail had won the race by .01 second over Juliet Cuthbert. "I wouldn't wish my disease on anyone," Gail said afterward. "But now I know there is no obstacle that I cannot get over." Later, Gail added, "I knew I was back!" For her victory, she was named the "World's Fastest Woman," the title that usually

Photo finish: Gail (in lane two) edges out Juliet Cuthbert of Jamaica in the 100-meter finals.

goes to the winner of the Olympic 100-meter race.

As Gail took her victory lap around the Olympic stadium, she remembered: "I was thinking, 'A year ago, you couldn't walk. Now, you're running. You've just won the gold.'"

While Gail was enjoying her Olympic gold medal, however, a shadow suddenly descended over her victory. One of the other runners, Gwen Torrence, had accused three of her competitors, including Gail, of using performance-enhancing drugs. The same types of accusations had occurred in past Olympics. Beginning in 1968, the Olympic movement began testing athletes for these drugs. In some cases, athletes had tested positive for illegal performance-enhancing drugs and were disqualified. After the 1988 games, for example, the Canadian track and field star Ben Johnson was stripped of his medals for using steroids. But suspicions could easily swirl around other athletes who were completely innocent.

Gail denied ever using performance-enhancing drugs. Her coach, Bobby Kersee, was very upset that any accusation would be made against her. "Did somebody say one of my athletes isn't clean?" he asked angrily. "Gail Devers has been tested almost as much as my wife [Jackie Joyner-Kersee] in the out-of-competition program."

Olympic athletes must undergo two types of drug testing. One type occurs after an athletic competition. Athletes are immediately notified that they must produce a urine sample that will be tested for the presence of drugs. Another type of testing occurs outside of competition. These are surprise tests, and athletes have no notice that they will occur. But, in either case, an athlete who tests positive for drugs may be banned from competition or disqualified if he or she has just competed in an event.

In an attempt to clear up the accusations of drug use in 1992, the International Olympic Committee stated two days after the 100-meter final that in tests administered on the women in the race there had been no positive results for drugs. Torrence was still unrepentant. As she said of Gail: "If she's mad, it doesn't bother me. We

Gwen Torrence (right) hugs Jamaican runner Merlene Ottey after winning the 200-meter event in Barcelona. Torrence, whom Gail Devers beat in the 100-meter competition, accused Gail and others of using performance-enhancing drugs.

weren't friendly to begin with." Ironically, the first person Gail had kissed after winning the 100-meter sprint was Gwen Torrence, her teammate. But Gail couldn't spend too much time worrying about Torrence's problems. She had another race to run—the 100-meter hurdles. This was her premier event, and everyone expected her to win the gold medal. In the first qualifying

Gail tumbled to the ground after catching her foot on the final hurdle in the 100-meter hurdles. A gold-medal hopeful in the event, she took her fifth-place finish in stride.

round, however, she finished a disappointing third, then effortlessly won the second round.

As the finals began, Gail seemed to fly out of the starting blocks. She appeared to float over the first nine hurdles, opening up a long lead of several meters. Gail was about to win her second gold medal. Then disaster struck. Gail's lead leg hit the 10th hurdle and she stumbled, falling onto the ground. "I never got to the 10th hurdle that fast," Gail said afterward. "I hit it with my lead leg and couldn't recover. I was fighting to stay on my feet. I lost the battle." Somehow she managed to crawl across the finish line. But it was too little, too late. Gail finished fifth. "It just wasn't meant to be," she remarked stoically.

But Gail had won the most impressive victory of her

life. She had battled back from a debilitating disease to win the greatest prize in sports—an Olympic gold medal. What was it about this 25-year-old athlete that gave her such stamina, such a will to win? "Whenever faced with a challenge, I dig deep within myself and summon my spiritual and physical forces," she said. "This gives me the focus, determination, perseverance and support I need to succeed."

Gail is a picture of concentration as she stands in the starting blocks during a practice session at UCLA.

2

BEGINNING
TO RACE

YOLANDA GAIL DEVERS was born on November 19, 1966, in Seattle, Washington. As she grew up, both parents worked at jobs that involved helping other people. Her father, Larry, was a Baptist minister; her mother, Alabe, was a teacher's aide in an elementary school. When Gail was still a child, the family moved to National City, California, outside of San Diego.

"From kindergarten on through high school, Gail was the kind who never wanted to miss a day of class," her father recalled. "Doing well in school was her foundation." But Gail's parents didn't push her too hard. "We were a *Leave It to Beaver* family," Gail recalled, referring to a popular television program about a happy American family of the 1950s. "We had picnics, rode bikes and played touch football together. We did Bible studies together."

By the time Gail was 10 years old, she had decided to become an elementary school teacher. She even practiced tutoring her friends with some of her mother's instructional books. As she entered adolescence,

A view of San Diego. Gail's family moved near the Southern California city when she was a child.

she was not a rebellious child. Her brother, however, seemed to be a rebel. The children were expected to be home before dark, but her older brother was intent on staying out longer. "I would be a little mother, tugging him in, explaining to him that later he'd understand," Gail explained. "My mom says I've always been old."

When Gail entered Sweetwater High School, she had no plans to become a track star. "It was my brother's fault," she recalled. "He played football, and during my sophomore year he had me work out with the cross-country team to get in shape with him." Her brother had always teased her, Gail recalled, that she couldn't run as fast as he did. So she started practicing and began entering events during the track season. Gail competed in a middle-distance race, the 800 meters, and much to everyone's surprise she set a California Intramural Federation (CIF) record. "From then on, running was all that mattered," Gail said. "I had found my stride."

Friends and coaches at Sweetwater High suggested that Gail try out for other events. So she competed in the 300-meter and 400-meter hurdles, setting CIF records in San Diego. Gene Alim, her high school track coach, remembered that he never had to push Gail or set any goals for her; she did these things for herself. "No matter what, she was going to be college scholarship material," he said. "We just didn't want her to stress out on the competition."

But they didn't need to worry. Gail Devers loved track and field and she became the greatest athlete in Sweetwater history. She won 3 state titles, 4 Southern California regional titles, and 12 San Diego intramural titles. In her high school yearbook, senior Gail Devers was honored with the words: "Gail, a model of an Olympian." She wrote: "Follow your dreams." Gail always had dreams and believed that with hard work they could be realized.

Gail's dreams took her to UCLA, a college she chose because there were top athletes there and she felt the competition would help sharpen her skills as a track star. She had also heard about a new coach of women's track there named Robert Kersee.

Gail Devers was preceded by a long line of great female Olympic track stars, some of whom may have been her role models. When she went to UCLA, she would train under a coach who had already achieved enormous success. Bobby Kersee is considered one of the world's best track and field coaches. Not only that,

Part of the UCLA campus. Gail was determined to continue the school's tradition of producing world-class track athletes.

he is renowned as an expert on physical fitness. In addition to training and coaching female track and field stars, Kersee has worked with elite athletes in other sports. For example, he helped St. Louis Cardinals baseball slugger Ray Lankford recover from knee surgery. He also helped tennis star Monica Seles overcome physical injuries.

Brian Jordan of the Atlanta Braves, who also worked with Kersee, explained his approach this way: "Bobby is all about tough love because he knows you have the potential to take it to the next level." Kersee combines great concern for his athletes with a hard-driving approach designed to bring out the best in them.

Kersee was born in the Canal Zone, Panama, and attended high school in San Pedro, California. In 1978, he earned a degree in physical education at California

Jackie Joyner-Kersee celebrates her victory in the long jump at the 1988 Seoul Olympics with her coach and husband, Bob Kersee.

State University–Long Beach, and began coaching at California State University–Northridge. From there he went to UCLA, where he trained Jackie Joyner, who would become his wife in 1986. In 1984, she competed in the heptathlon at the Los Angeles Olympics. The heptathlon is a two-day competition that includes seven different events: 100-meter hurdles, high jump, shot put, 200-meter race, long jump, javelin, and finally the 800-meter race. The athlete with the highest combined score for all the events is declared the winner. Joyner won a silver medal in Los Angeles. Then, four years later, she went to the games in Seoul and won a gold medal in the heptathlon and the long jump. She won the gold medal again in the heptathlon at the Olympics four years later.

Like Gail, Joyner also suffered from a potentially

Like Gail, Florence Griffith Joyner, seen here taking a victory lap after a race, saw her career threatened by health concerns. Joyner learned to manage her asthma very effectively.

career-ending illness. In her case, it was asthma. But she overcame this illness to become, in the opinion of sports experts, the greatest female athlete of all time.

Another track star Kersee trained was Florence Griffith Joyner. "Flo-Jo," as she was called, won a silver medal at the 1984 Summer Olympics. Four years later, in Seoul, she showed herself to be track and field's top female sprinter by winning gold medals in the 100 meters and 200 meters, and capturing another medal in a relay.

Earlier, Kersee had coached Valerie Brisco-Hooks to three gold medals at the 1984 Summer Olympics. So even without Gail Devers, Kersee had firmly established his reputation, having coached three great female track and field champions.

As Gail recalled, "Don't ask me how—I had the idea that he was an old white man." Gail finally saw Kersee when she went to the Olympic trials in 1984. "He was easy to spot because he was screaming at the top of his lungs at Jackie Joyner. I said 'Uh-oh, maybe I can wait to meet him.'" When Gail entered UCLA in 1984, Joyner was the school's leading track star. That summer at the Olympics in Los Angeles, Joyner won a silver medal in the heptathlon. Although Gail showed outstanding promise during her freshman year in the 400-meter hurdles, the 200 meters, and the 4 x 100-meter relay team, Joyner overshadowed everyone. But Kersee believed that Gail had enormous potential.

Kersee told Gail that she could make the 1988 Olympic team and even win a gold medal in 1992. "She looked at me," Kersee recalled, "strangely." Gail explained: "He had all these visions of years and years ahead. I could see he was crazy." But Gail listened. "I thought if he had all this faith in me, he'd coach me well. For quite a while Bobby believed in me more than I believed in myself."

Gail trained rigorously. She went on a diet that included no beef or junk food, but plenty of fish and chicken. But she couldn't stay off ice cream and allowed herself a dish once a week. Under Kersee's guidance, Gail learned how to use her head to run a smart 100-meter race. She divided it into three zones. In the first 40 meters, she tried to get a fast start out of the blocks and really pick up speed. In the second 40 meters, she stayed focused and took control of the race. In the last 20 meters, she would try to use quick, short strides that would take her across the finish line a winner.

But Gail did not stick with only a single event. As a sophomore she won the 100- and 200-meter races and the long jump, and she participated on relay teams. Despite her triumphs, Gail stayed humble. "I attribute my success to God," she said.

As a junior at UCLA, Gail continued to compete in a wide range of events, believing that all the competition helped sharpen her abilities as a track star. "I'll quit the day I don't have fun," she said. "I try not to put any pressure on myself. I don't feel I have to win every race. . . . That's when you start messing up." Kersee agreed. He realized that Gail was so highly motivated that he didn't have to set goals for her. She did that for herself.

In 1987, she achieved first place in six events in the Pacific 10 Championships, including the 100 and 200 meters and the 100-meter hurdles. The pace, however, didn't seem to exhaust Gail, who loved the competition. "It doesn't tire me out mentally or physically," she said. Gail always liked the 100-meter race because it was short. When she tried the 100-meter hurdles, however, many people predicted that she'd never compete at the highest levels, despite her blazing speed. The reason? Her height: at just five feet four inches she was considered too short to clear the hurdles without breaking stride. But Gail proved the doubters wrong. Kersee attributed much of Gail's success to her tremendous lower-body strength, her speed, and her long arms, which he likened to spaghetti.

As a senior, Gail set a new American record in the 100-meter hurdles—12.71 seconds. In May 1988, UCLA competed against its arch rival, the University of Southern California (USC). In the big meet, Gail shone. She won the long jump with a leap of 21 feet 9½ inches, captured the 100 meters, and outclassed the field in the 100-meter hurdles. Asked about Gail, Kersee said: "I'm sure glad she decided to come to UCLA. My No. 1 goal is to keep her healthy."

In May, Gail competed in the Pacific Coast Conference Championship, where she recorded two impressive victories.

She ran away with the 100-meter hurdles, recording the fastest time for an American woman. And, in winning the 100-meter sprint, she recorded the second-best time in the world.

Despite putting so much effort into her athletic career, Gail found time for a social life. Shortly after her amazing performance against USC, she was married to fellow UCLA track star Ron Roberts. But there wasn't much time for a honeymoon. The Seoul Olympics awaited.

At the U.S. Olympic Trials, Gail qualified for the American Olympic team by finishing second in the 100-meter hurdles. But after she traveled to South Korea and began training in Seoul, something happened. "I suffered migraine headaches, sleeplessness, fainting spells and frequent vision loss," she recalled. "I should have been at my peak performance. Instead, I was constantly exhausted and my body felt out of control." At first, Gail thought it was simply the pressure of training. But she had no strength. In the quarterfinal qualifying race at Seoul, she could finish no better than fourth. In the semifinals, she was the last person to cross the finish line, finishing eighth. Gail wouldn't be running for a medal in the finals.

After all of her previous success, Gail found it extremely disappointing to leave Seoul without even a bronze medal. Kersee blamed himself for failing to prepare her properly for the grueling test of Olympic competition. But the reality turned out to be something quite different— and far more serious. Gail's health continued to grow worse. It looked as if she might never compete again.

Graves' disease took a huge toll on Gail. She became too weak to walk, and the strain created by the disease ultimately led to her divorce.

3

GRAVES' DISEASE

GAIL LOOKED TERRIBLE. Her weight, which was usually about 120 pounds, fluctuated wildly between 140 and under 90. At times she appeared to be suffering from anorexia. But friends speculated that she might have a drug problem or even be stricken with AIDS. Gail had no strength in her body. She couldn't sprint; indeed, she could barely walk. "Bobby would tell me to go to the other side of the track and bring a hurdle or something. I'd get there and not remember what I was there for," Gail recalled.

Her hair was also falling out. "Each day it got worse: it kept coming out in patches," she remembered. Gail was very proud of her finger-nails; in fact, in running circles, she was known for her long nails and for the bright nail polish she painted on them. But her nails had become extremely brittle, breaking easily and failing to grow back.

At first, doctors couldn't diagnose her illness. They thought it might be stress from the tough training schedule that Gail followed to prepare her for the Olympics. But she wasn't convinced.

"The hardest part was not knowing—being undiagnosed for so long," she said. "I mean, I felt something was wrong with me, but people kept telling me there was nothing wrong. But I KNEW. I kept saying 'No, these things aren't adding up.' " Further examination led doctors to guess that she might be suffering from diabetes—a disease in which the body's liver doesn't properly metabolize sugar. But that was eventually ruled out.

Meanwhile, Gail was having other symptoms. Her skin was peeling off in layers. Gail, who always strives to be attractive in public, couldn't even look at herself in the mirror. In fact, she covered all the mirrors in her house. "I didn't want to look at myself and I'd refer to myself as the 'alligator woman,' " she recalls. She tried to avoid going out in public and stayed at home for days on end in a darkened room. In addition, her eyes began bulging, and she was often unable to see out of her left eye. A swelling had also developed under her neck. The condition, called goiter, was caused by an enlarged thyroid gland.

Finally, after more than two years, her doctors realized that Gail had developed hyperthyroidism, also called Graves' disease. Robert Graves, an Irish physician, was the first scientist to describe this type of illness. Graves' disease is caused by a malfunction of the body's immune system. As a result, chemicals called antibodies overstimulate the cells in the thyroid gland. This gland, which is located in the neck, regulates the rate at which the body's cells produce energy. If the thyroid gland does not operate properly, it can result in hypothyroidism (an underactive thyroid) or hyperthyroidism (an overactive thyroid).

Gail was suffering from an overactive thyroid. Scientists believe that the onset of Graves' disease may be triggered by stress, such as the conditions under which Gail was preparing for the 1988 Olympics, her first major international competition. About four to eight times more women than men suffer from Graves' disease. Yet, in a recent Louis Harris poll of 1,000 women, most didn't

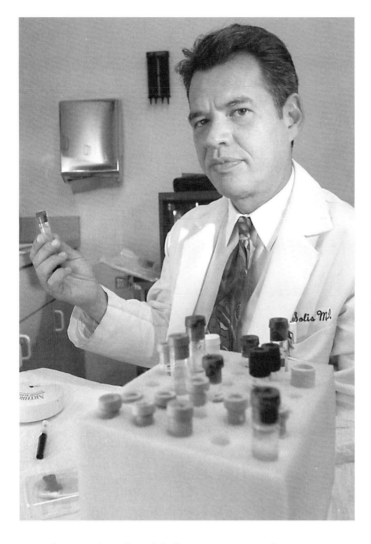

A doctor holds a sample of blood he will test for thyroid dysfunction. Experts estimate that more than 20 million Americans suffer from some form of thyroid disease.

even know what thyroid disease was or what symptoms it included. "No woman should have to suffer what I went through," Gail says, "and hopefully, she won't if she knows to look for the signs and symptoms of thyroid disorder."

The symptoms of Graves' disease include heart palpitations, hair loss, tiredness, and variations in menstrual flow. The disease is also associated with inflammation and bulging of the eyes, called exophthalmos, as well as goiter.

A physiotherapist attends to Gail during a training session. She returned to the top of her sport despite incredible obstacles.

It strikes a small number of women, usually between the ages of 20 and 40.

At first, doctors treated Gail with radiation therapy. She began to feel better and eventually started jogging. But the jogging produced blood blisters on her feet. She went to a podiatrist who diagnosed the problem as too much stress and prescribed a foot ointment. But the condition became worse. "My feet swelled so people thought I was wearing five pairs of socks," she recalled. "I went out and bought men's house slippers, size 11 and 12. I cried the whole time. It was so bad I crawled to the bathroom."

Gail couldn't continue caring for herself, so her mother began living in Gail's house and nursing her. "She carried me to the bathroom," says Gail. "I had gone back to the infant stage." Doctors feared cancer and even considered amputating both of Gail's feet. Then they realized that the radiation treatments were the cause of much of Gail's suffering. The doctors stopped the radiation and put Gail on antithyroid drugs. These drugs, which include propylthiouracil and methimazole, reduce the amount of hormones that the thyroid gland produces. Sometimes there can be unpleasant side effects, such as skin rashes, which Gail experienced.

"The hardest part is not having a thyroid disorder—it's not knowing," Gail explained. "The biggest thrill for me was finding out that I had something wrong, because I finally knew that I wasn't crazy. . . . With lots of hard work, determination, perseverance, and faith in God, I was able to . . . regain my health."

Gradually, Gail could begin training again. She still dreamed of getting another shot at an Olympic medal at the Seoul Games. "Everyone has obstacles to overcome," Gail said. "No matter how hopeless things may seem, never give up on yourself." Gail never did and eventually she became an Olympic champion.

The Panathenian Stadium in Athens, Greece, was the site of the first modern Olympic Games, which were held in 1896. Women did not participate until four years later in Paris, France.

4

WOMEN AND THE OLYMPIC GAMES

THE OLYMPICS TRACE their origins to the ancient world. They began in Greece about 776 B.C. with only one event—a race of about 170 meters. The Olympic Games continued for approximately 1,200 years, but only men were allowed to compete. Then the games disappeared for centuries as Europe fell into chaos with the collapse of the Roman Empire.

The modern Olympics were revived during the 1890s. In 1894, the International Olympic Committee (IOC) was created in Paris, France. The IOC governs the Olympic movement and selects host cities for the Summer and Winter Games. In 1896 the first modern Olympics were held in Athens, Greece.

Still, women did not compete until 1900, when the Olympic Games were held in Paris. In this Olympics, women were restricted to certain events that were considered "ladylike." These included golf and tennis. In Paris, an American woman named Margaret Abbott won a gold medal in golf. With her picture-perfect swing,

Abbott had won tournaments in Chicago, her hometown, as well as other cities in the United States, before her triumph in Paris.

It was not until the 1928 Olympic Games in Amsterdam, Holland, that women began competing in track and field events. Up until this time, the uniform for track stars was considered too skimpy and revealing for women to wear in public. But during the 1920s women achieved not only the right to vote in the United States but greater freedom to wear what they wanted and conduct their personal lives as they pleased.

At Amsterdam there were six events for women—the discus, the high jump, the 100-meter and 200-meter sprints, a relay race, and an 800-meter run. Unfortunately, some of the female athletes collapsed at the finish line of the 800-meter race. The IOC, believing the 800 meters too tough for women, removed the event from succeeding Olympics; not until 1960 did women again compete at that distance. But at least one American woman at the 1928 Games proved that she had what it took for Olympic competition. Betty Robinson, from Riverdale, Illinois, became the first woman to win a gold medal in track when she crossed the finish line ahead of the other runners in the 100-meter race.

Perhaps the most famous female athlete of the period, however, was an American named Mildred "Babe" Didrikson. Indeed, she has been called the greatest woman athlete of the first part of the 20th century. In 1932, Didrikson won events at the U.S. national track and field championships. Then she went on to the 1932 Olympic Games in Los Angeles. Not one to underestimate her own abilities, she said, "I came out here to beat everybody in sight, and that is exactly what I am going to do."

Didrikson proved as good as her promises. She won a gold medal in the javelin event and set a world record on the way to winning the 80-meter hurdles. She also won a

Olympic gold medalist Mildred "Babe" Didrikson jumps a hurdle. At the 1932 Olympics in Los Angeles she set a record in the 80-meter hurdles.

silver medal in the high jump. It was a very impressive performance.

Four years later, in the Olympics at Berlin, Germany, another American woman made headlines. Like Gail Devers, Betty Robinson had nearly seen her career end prematurely. In 1931 Robinson sustained serious injuries in an airplane accident, and it seemed unlikely that she would ever run again. But she recovered, trained hard, and participated on the women's relay team in 1936. The Americans defeated the Germans, and Robinson won a gold medal.

Unlike other athletic events, the Olympics showcase not only individual athletes but the countries they represent as well. And during the 1936 Berlin Games, politics nearly overshadowed athletics. The host country, Germany, was controlled by Adolf Hitler and his Nazi Party, which preached the superiority of the German Aryan race. Hitler hoped that the Olympics would prove his racial theories as German athletes swept the gold medals. The Nazi dictator was disappointed, however; not only did the American women win the relay event, but another great American sprinter named Helen Stephens won the 100-meter race. Meanwhile, in the men's competition, the great American track and field star Jesse Owens won gold medals in the 100 meters, the 200 meters, and the long jump. This was a special blow to Hitler because Owens was black —supposedly an inferior race.

Three years after the Berlin Games, Hitler and the Nazis would ignite World War II, which prevented the Olympic Games from being held in 1940 and 1944. In 1948, an African-American woman named Alice Coachman was named a member of the U.S. Olympic team. At the Olympic Games in London, Coachman competed in the high jump. She became the only member of the U.S. women's team to win a gold medal, and the first African-American woman to receive this award.

But an even more famous African-American athlete, Wilma Rudolph, would overshadow Coachman. Rudolph attended Tennessee State University, where she broke records in many of her track meets. Then, in 1960, she competed in the Olympic Games held in Rome. As one reporter put it: "From the moment she first sped down the track in Rome's Olympic Stadium, there was no doubt she was the fastest woman the world had ever seen." Rudolph won three gold medals—in the 100 meters, the 200 meters,

At the 1948 London Games, Alice Coachman became the first black female to capture a gold medal, winning the high jump. Coachman never lost a high-jump competition between 1939 and 1948.

and the 4 x 100-meter relay. Along the way she shattered Olympic and world track records.

Four years later another student at Tennessee State, Wyomia Tyus, would excel at the Olympics. A champion in the 100-meter dash, Tyus went to the 1964 Olympics in Tokyo, Japan. There she won a gold medal with an incredible finish, recording a time of 11.4 seconds. But this would not be her only victory. In 1968, she

*Joan Benoit waves to the crowd
moments after crossing the finish
line to win the gold medal in
the women's marathon at the
1984 Los Angeles Olympics.*

competed again—this time, at the Olympic Games in Mexico City. Here Tyus again won the 100-meter dash, becoming the first person to accomplish that feat.

In 1984, at the Los Angeles Olympic Games, women were allowed to compete for the first time in the marathon, an endurance race of 26.2 miles. For many years, it was thought that women did not have the stamina for such a long race. At Los Angeles, the marathon belonged to Joan Benoit, of Cape Elizabeth, Maine, almost from the start. She opened up a big lead on the field early in the race and never looked back. "I was so charged up that when I broke the tape, I could have turned around and run another twenty-six miles," Benoit said.

For any great track and field star, the road to an Olympic medal presents a long and grueling challenge. Like Gail Devers, athletes maintain an arduous training schedule throughout high school and college. This training prepares them to compete in the premier events in track and field. The International Amateur Athletic Federation sponsors many of these events.

Founded in 1912 in Stockholm, Sweden, the IAAF is the governing body for track and field throughout the world. The IAAF certifies all international records and sponsors important meets, such as the World Championships and World Indoor Championships. From many years, only unpaid athletes could compete in IAAF events. But starting in 1985, the organization permitted athletes to be paid for such things as product endorsements. However, athletes could not control the money they earned while they were still competing. Instead, all earnings would go into a trust fund administered by the IAAF.

In addition to winning IAAF events, athletes who go to the Olympics must be certified by their own National Olympic Committees (NOCs). Thus an individual athlete cannot enter the Olympics on his or her own but must be selected to be a member of a national team, such as the United States Olympic team. Generally, making the U.S. Olympic track team is a two-phase process. First, the athlete must excel in high-level competition, winning events or posting excellent times (or, in field events, heights or distances). That earns the athlete an invitation to the U.S. Olympic Team Trials for Track and Field. If the athlete places first or second at the trials, he or she automatically qualifies for the Olympics.

The IAAF and the various NOCs also conduct drug testing to ensure that an athlete is not using performance-enhancing drugs. Urine samples of athletes are taken before and after the U.S. Olympic trials. Any athlete who tests positive for drugs can be barred from the team. The

United States Olympic Committee is very clear about its standards: It wants only the most exemplary athletes to represent their country at the Olympics.

For an Olympic athlete, winning a gold medal is the ultimate accomplishment. But sometimes, the moment of triumph is overshadowed by accusations of cheating through the use of performance-enhancing drugs. As noted earlier, for example, in 1992 Gail Devers and other female track and field stars were accused of using drugs to win their medals. Testing by Olympic authorities, however, revealed no banned substances in the athletes' systems. Of course, it is possible to beat even the most sensitive drug test, according to experts. Thus, an accusation of doping can dog an athlete for years even if that athlete has never tested positive for a banned substance and is, in fact, clean. Unfortunately, proving to skeptics beyond the shadow of a doubt that an athlete *is* clean is next to impossible.

Proving the opposite isn't that difficult, as the world found out at the 1998 Summer Games in Seoul. After demolishing a strong 100-meter field that included world record holder Carl Lewis, the Canadian track star Ben Johnson saw his gold medal taken away after a postrace urine test revealed the presence of a performance-enhancing drug called stanozolol. Johnson was also banned from competition by the International Amateur Athletic Federation. After trying to mount a comeback several years later, Johnson once more tested positive for banned substances and never achieved victory again.

Stanozolol is an anabolic steroid, a kind of hormone that, experts believe, has been widely abused by athletes whose events require explosive speed or strength. Anabolic steroids enable athletes to train harder and recover faster, increasing the size and strength of muscles. While they won't transform an average athlete into a world-beater, at the highest levels of competition even a small edge can make the difference between

standing atop the winner's podium and watching the medal ceremony from the stands.

Steroids aren't completely synthetic substances; the human body produces its own steroids naturally. In males, one of the most important of these is a hormone called testosterone. During puberty, the male testes naturally produce increased amounts of testosterone. Testosterone is responsible for helping adolescent boys develop larger muscles, grow facial hair, and get a deeper voice.

Canada's Ben Johnson (center) is surrounded by members of the press at the Kimpo Airport in Seoul, South Korea, after being stripped of his Olympic gold medal in the 100-meter dash.

As part of their training, some male athletes may take large doses of testosterone to enhance their muscle development. Testosterone can be injected directly into the bloodstream, be taken as a pill, or both. Small amounts of testosterone have little effect, because so much of the hormone naturally exists inside the male body. Male athletes must take megadoses to create an increase in muscle size. This can give an elite athlete an edge that may be enough for victory, especially in events like the 100-meter dash, which are decided by hundredths of a second.

Female athletes naturally produce some testosterone in their bodies, but far less of it than males. By using steroids, women can greatly increase the size of their muscles and achieve an advantage in athletic competition. During the 1960s and 1970s, East German women swimmers and track stars routinely used steroids during training, helping them develop the strength to win numerous gold medals during the Olympics.

In 1973 the International Olympic Committee (IOC) banned steroids. Nevertheless, some athletes—often under the direction of their coaches and team doctors, as in the case of the East Germans—continued to use them, relying on sophisticated regimes to beat drug tests. (Much is known about the use of banned substances in East Germany's sports programs because after the collapse of the country's Communist government and reunification with West Germany, records from that program were made public.) Other athletic groups, such as the National Football League and the National Collegiate Athletic Association, also banned steroids. Yet, according to some estimates, 5 to 15 percent of adult athletes still use steroids, such as testosterone, during training to enhance their performance in competition.

While steroids may give an athlete some immediate advantage, the long-term effects can be extremely dangerous. Male and female athletes who use steroids are at greater risk for heart attack. Steroids also prevent the development of high-density lipoproteins (HDL), sometimes known as "good cholesterol." HDL can help prevent arteries from becoming blocked by lipoproteins that can cause strokes and heart attacks. Among women, the use of steroids can also lead to the growth of facial hair, lowering of the voice, and even baldness—typical male characteristics. None of these characteristics can be changed.

Some athletes also believe that steroids produce a symptom known as "'roid rage"—basically excessive aggressiveness. Male athletes who have abused steroids report starting fights with friends and even physically abusing their spouses as a result of the extra testosterone.

In the past, urine testing after an athletic event was often not sophisticated enough to detect residual traces of steroids that the athlete had used weeks or months before, during training. More sensitive tests have been developed, however.

Unfortunately, making it harder to get away with using steroids simply makes some athletes who are inclined to cheat seek another substance that will give them an unfair edge. Another banned substance that began to be abused is human growth hormone. This drug enlarges the body's cartilage and ligaments that connect bones and muscles. If muscles become too large (as can happen through overtraining or abuse of steroids), an athlete's cartilage or ligaments may be more easily ripped or torn. This problem can be avoided by the use of growth hormone.

Another widely abused class of drugs are stimulants. Especially popular are amphetamines and ephedrines. Stimulants enable an athlete's body to become more alert and work harder. Stimulants activate the sympathetic nervous system (SNS), which galvanizes us into action when we need to respond to stress and deliver a peak performance. The pupils of our eyes become dilated so we can see more around us. Our heart pumps more rapidly, sending more blood to our muscles so we can do more work. We take in more oxygen, which is rushed to our body's cells to burn food faster and produce more energy.

Amphetamines stimulate all of these responses. Some athletes use amphetamines to improve concentration during training; others rely on them for an extra burst of energy on the day of a competition. Unfortunately, amphetamines are highly addictive and can cause heart damage as well as stroke.

Another type of stimulant is ephedrine, which is often taken as a drug called Ma Huang or "herbal ecstasy." According to some experts, herbal ecstasy is "one of the most widely marketed performance-enhancing drugs. Its use by athletes is skyrocketing." Like amphetamines, ephedrine is banned by the IOC. Nevertheless, some athletes have been caught taking it and disqualified from competition.

In addition to stimulants, the IOC also bans another class of drugs called beta-blockers. These have the reverse effect of stimulants. Beta-blockers are designed to block the natural action of the SNS, which often makes an athlete feel anxious and jittery before competition. This is the reaction most of us experience before a stressful event. For an athlete, however, nerves can get in the way of turning in a top performance. Beta-blockers are designed to help athletes feel cool and calm as they prepare to compete.

Although random testing of elite athletes during training and urine testing right after competition probably catches most cheaters who use performance-enhancing drugs, experts concede that a foolproof test for all banned substances is still many years from becoming a reality. The chemical signatures that banned substances produce after the body metabolizes them can be masked with other drugs or with certain diets or other procedures.

In spite of the best efforts of the IOC, the IAAF, and individual nations' Olympic governing bodies, an estimated 1 to 2 percent of Olympic athletes still use banned performance-enhancing substances—and get away with it.

Gail celebrates winning a gold medal in the 100-meter hurdles at the 1993 World Athletics Championships. Her incredible speed is the result of intense training and great natural talent.

5

MIND AND BODY

OLYMPIC TRACK AND field includes a variety of competitive events, each of which is contested by the best athletes from dozens of countries. These championship games take place inside a huge stadium that seats tens of thousands of spectators. Some of the events occur on a 400-meter, oval-shaped track. These include the 100-meter and 200-meter sprints, the 100- and 400-meter hurdles, relay races, and longer track events, like the 1,500-, 3,000-, and 5,000-meter races. Meanwhile, inside the oval other athletes are competing in field events—such as the pole vault, high jump, javelin throw, shot put, and long jump.

Gail's specialties are sprints and hurdles. To succeed in these events—which may be decided in little more time than it takes to read this sentence—a competitor must be willing to put in years of arduous training. In an interview with *Science World* magazine, Gail explained her daily routine. Early in the morning she begins with 100-meter sprints that continue for three hours. After a light meal, she sprints for two additional hours. Then she works out in the weight room for three hours in the afternoon. "My friends tease me because I only know one speed—fast," Gail revealed. "I run fast, talk fast, even sleep fast!"

Her practice sprints develop more blood vessels in Gail's leg muscles. These bring more oxygen to her legs, which creates greater energy and faster speeds on the track. As *Science World* points out, weightlifting "strengthens skeletal muscles . . . such as biceps and quadriceps. They are attached to your bones and control all voluntary movements, like walking, running and bending." The majority of Gail's muscles are composed of long cells, known as fast-twitch fibers. These are excellent for sprinting because they rapidly get smaller and longer, helping sprinters achieve great bursts of speed over a short distance.

To prepare for the hurdles, Gail works on her timing. She must take each of the 10 hurdles in stride, without catching her front or back leg. Then she must land on the ground and continue running at full speed until she reaches the next hurdle.

What makes a star athlete is not only physical prowess but also intelligence. Tiger Woods, for example, has been successful in part because of his flawless golf swing. But he has also mastered the "head" game of golf. He remains cool, carefully thinks through each shot, and always remains focused.

Gail is the same. For example, she doesn't simply accept what Bobby Kersee tells her; she thinks carefully about it. "I'm one of those 'question' people," she explains. "I always ask why."

"I don't like to be questioned," Kersee responds, "but I welcome a serious request for the reason behind a given workout or technique."

When she was in high school, Gail was a middle-distance runner, competing in the 800 meters. Unlike the sprints, these races require a constant infusion of energy over a longer period. Gail needed stamina to go the

Gail specializes in sprints and hurdles. Timing and technique are especially critical in the latter event.

distance. Long-distance runners, like marathoner Joan Benoit, must build up the slow-twitch fibers in their legs. These fibers are especially built for the slower pace that a marathoner must maintain over a long race. If a marathon runner starts too fast, she may run out of energy before the race is over. Successful marathon racers always keep energy in reserve for the end of the race to take them to the finish line.

Sprinters, like Gail, begin a race by pushing off against two starting blocks. These consist of a metal bar with a pair of adjustable footpads. When a starter says, "On your marks," Gail leans forward with her hands on the ground behind the starting line. On the word "set," she raises her hips and leans forward. Sometimes a racer will leave the blocks before the signal to start the race is given. Then the racers must take their positions again. Once the starter's gun fires, the racers explode out of the starting blocks and sprint down the track. Middle- and long-distance racers usually begin from a standing start, then begin running when the gun sounds.

In addition to sprints, Gail also runs in relay races. In contrast to other track competitions, these are team events, with four runners on each relay team. As a runner finishes her leg of the race, she must pass a baton—a hollow tube made out of wood, plastic, or metal and about a foot long—to the next member of the team. Particularly in shorter relay races such as the 4 x 100 (which is only once around the track), good baton exchanges are crucial. The idea is for the runner accepting the baton to be in full stride at the time of the exchange. But the exchange must occur in the designated area or the team is disqualified. Many a relay has been lost because a runner underestimated how tired her teammate finishing a leg was and sprinted out too fast. On the other hand, runners making an exchange have been known to collide because the one accepting the baton went out too slowly. And sometimes the runners simply fumble the baton while trying to make the exchange.

Earlier in her career, Gail also participated in field events, such as the triple jump and the long jump. In the triple jump, a competitor races down a runway, increasing her speed as she goes. When she reaches the take-off board, she takes a "hop, step, and jump." For the final jump, the athlete lands in a sandy pit. The triple jump requires coordination, timing, and leaping ability, as well as good speed.

By contrast, the long jump, which was a better event for Gail, is more suited to pure sprinters. Only by hitting the take-off board with a great deal of speed can a competitor launch herself into the air and, legs striding all the time, fly above the sand pit for a long distance.

Gail, who possessed a solid work ethic to go along with tremendous natural talent, may well have been able to excel in a number of track and field events. But she chose to specialize in the 100 meters and the 100-meter hurdles, a difficult and unusual combination at the highest levels of competition. By 1992, having recovered from her disappointment in Seoul and her battle with Graves' disease, Gail tested herself in those events against the best in the world—and showed she had the stuff of champions.

Determined to take home two gold medals in the 1996 Summer Olympics, Gail put her blazing speed on display in Atlanta. She easily advanced beyond this qualifying heat for the 100-meter dash.

6

ON TO ATLANTA

OCTOBER 19, 1992, was a special day in National City, California. Mayor George H. Waters had declared it "Gail Devers Day" to honor the city's hometown girl for her victory at the Olympics. There was a parade, and the stadium at Sweetwater High School was named after Gail. She spoke to a large audience of students at Sweetwater, recalling her battle with Graves' disease and how she had bounced back to win the gold medal. "If I can leave you with anything," she told them, "have your dreams. But then you have to be willing to get out there and work for them too." It was vintage Gail—who always stresses the importance of setting personal goals and having the determination to achieve them. But no matter how famous she became, Gail never forgot where she came from and what she owed her parents as well as her coaches. One of the students, referring to Gail's return home, put it this way: "We're . . . glad she didn't forget her roots."

During 1993, Gail continued to compete in racing events. In

February, at the USA/Mobil Indoor Championships, she established a new American record for the 60-meter dash: 6.99 seconds. A few weeks later, she competed at the World Indoor Championships in Toronto, Canada. Her coach, Bobby Kersee, told her that it was one thing to win her first gold in the Olympics, but it might be much harder to win a second one in international competition. Kersee was challenging her to keep on winning. "He was just talking about how it's easy the first time," Gail explained. "He said it's harder to come back and repeat. It takes determination . . . will . . . mental toughness."

Although Kersee's athletes seem to love him, they also admit that he is a very demanding coach. As his wife, Jackie Joyner-Kersee, said in her autobiography, Bobby has an "overpowering desire to win" that can turn him into a "tyrannical, whirling dervish" when it comes to driving his athletes during training. "Bobby believes the key to perfect performance is perfect execution. . . . Along with discipline and proper technique, Bobby stressed mental preparation. One of his favorite expressions is, 'Those who know *why* will always beat those who know *how.*'"

Gail showed again that she had what it takes to win. In the 60-meter finals she won the race, beating the great Russian sprinter Irina Privalova. Gail's time was the second fastest in history.

"It's not hard for me to concentrate," Gail said about her impressive performance. "I definitely learned a lot from my illness. I'm stronger. I'm a more determined person. I don't think there's anything in my life that will come up that I can't get over."

In June, Gail won the 100-meter dash in the USA/Mobil Outdoor Championships in a time of 10.82 seconds. Later that summer, at the U.S. Olympic Festival events in San Antonio, Texas, she won the 100-meter

hurdles with a time of 12.76 seconds. Finally, she capped off the year in Stuttgart, Germany, in August, beating perennial rival Merlene Ottey of Jamaica to win the 100-meter race in the World Track & Field Championships. Her winning time of 10.81 seconds was .01 better than Ottey. Gail then went on to win the hurdles—becoming only the second person to achieve this double victory. For her success that year, she was voted the U.S. Olympic Committee's Sportswoman of the Year.

In 1994 Gail repeated in the USA Outdoor Championships with a victory in the 100-meter dash. But she

Gail competes in the 110-meter hurdles at the 1995 World Championships in Gothenburg, Sweden. She would leave that competition ranked number one in the world in the event.

was bothered by hamstring problems that year, and the nagging injuries prevented her from competing in the hurdles. Early in 1995, Gail was expected to compete against Gwen Torrence in the Millrose Games in New York City, but she had to withdraw because of another injury.

Once again, however, Gail bounced back, winning the 100-meter hurdles at the USA Outdoors in 1995. Although still bothered by injuries that year, she became the world champion in the hurdles at the championships in Gothenburg, Sweden, and was ranked number one in the world for that event. The 1996 Olympics in Atlanta were just around the corner, and Gail seemed on course to take two gold medals.

In May, however, Gail competed against Torrence once again and finished sixth. "I tore the calf muscle and had problems with my hamstring," she explained. In the U.S. Olympic trials, held in June, she seemed much better. In fact, Gail blew away the competition in several of her heats.

June also marked the first showing of a film on the Showtime network describing Gail's life. Called *Run for the Dream: The Gail Devers Story*, it chronicled her remarkable recovery from Graves' disease and her unforgettable win in the 100 meters at the 1992 Olympics. Now Gail had become a real celebrity. And, like other celebrities, she was flooded with product-endorsement offers. Indeed, she joined other Olympic gold medal winners, like Jackie Joyner-Kersee, whose heptathlon victory had led to endorsements for products such as Honda automobiles and McDonald's restaurants. In Atlanta during the 1996 Olympics, Gail's picture appeared on a billboard for Nike, the maker of athletic shoes.

The 1996 Summer Olympics marked the 100th anniversary of the modern Olympic Games. Athens

Jim Thorpe, seen here in his football uniform for the Carlisle (Pa.) Indian School, was stripped of his Olympic gold medals after it was learned that he had been paid to play baseball in 1909 and 1910. Today professional athletes may compete in Olympic events, and amateurs such as Gail Devers can make substantial sums of money through meet appearance fees and product endorsements.

had lobbied hard to be the host city for this milestone event—and the Greek capital offered a solid historical argument for its bid. Not only had Greece given the world the ancient Olympics, but Athens had hosted the first modern Olympics, in 1896. Despite this, Atlanta had won the honor of hosting the 1996 Summer Games.

Cities compete to host the Olympics not just for the prestige and publicity, but also for money. The Olympics draw hundreds of thousands of tourists, who pump a lot of cash into the local economy. Not only that, but television rights and sponsorships paid by large companies can be substantial. For example, the Atlanta Committee for the Olympic Games sold the TV rights to NBC for $456 million and obtained such official sponsors as Home Depot and Delta Airlines.

And for the athletes themselves, more than just the thrill of victory might be on the line. Each American gold medal winner at Atlanta would be awarded $15,000 from the USOC. In addition, winners might land lucrative product-endorsement deals from various companies.

The Atlanta Games saw 10,000 athletes from 197 countries compete in the events, which began with the lighting of the Olympic flame by former heavyweight boxing champion Muhammad Ali. For Gail these Olympics were special for several reasons. This time she wanted to win both the 100-meter dash and the 100-meter hurdles after falling short of that goal in Barcelona. Plus, now she could share the experience with her fiancé, Kenny Harrison, who was also competing. Harrison, a triple jumper, also shared Gail's coach, Bobby Kersee.

In the 100 meters, Gail once again found herself in an extremely close race for the gold medal. Her main competitor was Ottey of Jamaica, and the two hit the finish line almost together at 9.94 seconds. After reviewing photos of the finish, the judges awarded Gail the gold.

Meanwhile, Harrison was competing in the triple jump. "I told him, 'Don't you go out there . . . while

Kenny Harrison set an Olympic and American record with this triple jump of 59 feet, 4¼ inches during the 1996 Summer Games. Gail Devers, his fiancée, also struck gold in Atlanta.

I'm on the track,'" Gail said. She was afraid Harrison might distract her. But his competition had already begun. Harrison's longest jump was 59 feet, 4¼ inches, an Olympic record. He was competing while Gail was taking a victory lap around the stadium.

Now Gail would go for an Olympic double. If she could win a gold in the 100-meter hurdles, she would be the first woman to achieve this feat since Fannie Blankers-Koen in the 1948 Olympics. After missing the last hurdle in Barcelona, Gail had been working hard with Kersee to avoid a repeat. The coach had blamed himself for that mistake because he hadn't emphasized strongly enough to Gail that her stride pattern had to be different for the hurdles than it was for the 100-meter dash.

At Atlanta, Gail cleared all the hurdles, but three other runners beat her to the finish line. Ludmila Engquist of Sweden took the gold. For Gail, it was a great disappointment, but she seemed to take it in stride. She claimed that she just "never got into rhythm." And she added: "It just wasn't meant to be. But I finished fourth, better than I did in Barcelona. And I finished on my feet."

Later, she won another gold, for the 4 x 100 relay. Most of us would be thrilled just to compete in the Olympics. It's hard to imagine winning two gold medals and still being a little disappointed. But for Gail, like other world-class athletes, expectations are so much higher.

Millions of people found out about Gail Devers's remarkable story when they watched the television movie *Run for the Dream* in 1996. Charlayne Woodard played the role of Gail, while Robert Guillaume played her father, and Louis Gossett Jr. starred as Bobby Kersee. "Classy performances make this a standout," said *People* magazine; the *Boston Globe* called the film "inspiring." Perhaps one of the reasons the film rang true was that Gail had considerable input, serving as a producer for the show.

The film opens with Gail winning the 100-meter hurdles while still a student at UCLA. The camera comes in for a close-up on Gail's face, flushed with exhilaration at the thrill of crossing the finish line ahead of her competition.

Soon after her triumph, in mid-1988, Gail is married to Ron Roberts, a UCLA track star. While Gail dresses for the wedding, however, her mother notices that Gail has lost weight. It's the first sign that something is wrong with her health.

Gail competes in the U.S. Olympic Team trials and qualifies for the 1988 Olympic Games in Seoul, South Korea. But Bobby Kersee isn't happy with her performance. He expects her to finish first. Unknown to Gail, she has already begun to feel the effects of Graves' disease. Indeed, she can't run up a flight of stairs without getting out of breath.

As her gracious comments after finishing out of the medals in the 100-meter hurdles show, Gail handles media attention well. However, she guards her privacy closely.

As Gail continues preparing for the Olympics, her ability to run the hurdles is declining. "Do you want to win the gold?" Kersee asks her. Although Gail answers that she does, Kersee is afraid that somehow she won't be up to the task. As Gossett portrays him in the film, Kersee is a tough but inspirational coach who tries to convince Gail that she can be a champion athlete, but only by driving herself relentlessly. Later, Gail's husband asks her why she puts up with so much from Kersee. "He's the best track coach in the world," she tells him.

However, even Kersee can't make Gail run fast enough to overcome Graves' disease. The film portrays Gail combing her hair one morning and taking out a large clump of hair on her comb. She can't understand it. Then, after a warm-up on the track, Gail experiences severe pain while she is taking a shower. Gail is gripped by fear. "What's happening to me?" she wonders.

In Seoul, Gail fails to make it through the qualifying heat for the 100-meter hurdles. Knowing that something is wrong, she flies home to California. Gail, accompanied by her husband and her parents, goes from one doctor to another trying to find the cause of her illness. But they receive the same answer over and over again: It's stress, the doctors say; it's an emotional problem. They insist that something must be bothering Gail. Finally, Gail begins to believe that it is God's will that she stop running. In the film, however, Gail's husband believes the problem lies elsewhere. He believes that Kersee is the wrong coach for her and convinces Gail to leave him. Instead, Roberts becomes her coach. But he proves incapable of really helping her because he lacks Kersee's discipline and drive.

Meanwhile, Gail's ability to run is further sapped by her illness. Eventually, she finds a doctor who recognizes that it is more than just stress; it is Graves' disease. Her thyroid is "twice the size" of normal, the doctor tells her in the film, and it has to be brought down. Although she has a serious disease, Gail is relieved because someone has finally realized that the problem is not in her mind. But at first there seems to be little the doctor can do for her. As he tells Gail: "There is no cure." It looks like the end of her career, and Gail's disappointment is overwhelming.

Eventually, the doctor prescribes a course of treatment that includes radiation therapy. This is designed to shrink the thyroid, but the side effects are so powerful that Gail finds herself too exhausted to run. According to the film, Gail's estrangement from Kersee continues during this time. When he tries to comfort her during her illness, she turns away from him. Meanwhile, the radiation makes her even sicker. She refuses to take beta-blockers, which have been prescribed to reduce the impact of the radiation, because these drugs are banned by the IOC. The film presents a conflict between Kersee and Gail's husband. Roberts wants her to take the beta-blockers because he is convinced that she will never run again and never be tested by the IOC. But Kersee can't bring himself to agree; nor does Gail want to give up her dream of competing in the 1992 Olympics.

However, the radiation continues to make her feel worse. And even her strong faith in God is shaken. "Why does God hate me?" she asks her father in the television film. As Gail's health continues to decline, she locks herself in her house. The film shows her watching a track race won by her rival Gwen Torrence. Meanwhile, Gail is unable to walk and must drag herself across the floor because her feet are so swollen and blistered from the radiation. She is alone in the house because her husband has left her following repeated disagreements over her desire to keep running and her refusal to take the medication. When he eventually returns home, he finds her almost dead on the floor and is forced to rush her to the emergency room of the hospital. When Gail's parents blame him for not being constantly by her side during her illness, he leaves, never to return. Unfortunately, Roberts's inability to deal with Gail's illness or understand her desire to run again leads to their divorce.

Gail's recovery is slow, and she returns to her home in a wheelchair. But she hasn't lost her determination. In the most inspirational moment of the film, Kersee pays her a visit. Gail tells him that she wants to go to the Olympic Games in Barcelona, and Kersee says that he will get her tickets. Then she rises slowly from the wheelchair and stands on her feet. "I want to run in Barcelona," Gail tells him.

It is only 12 months to the Olympic trials and 18 months to the actual Olympic Games. Gail's wish seems impossible.

The television production depicts Gail's first tentative steps toward a return to racing. She arrives at the track in her wheelchair. She gets up and tries to walk, but the pain seems too much for her. When Gail wants to stop, it is Kersee who is there to encourage her onward. He recalls her past glory days as a runner in high school and college, urging her forward step by step. Gradually, Gail and Kersee work together to forge her comeback. Little by little her speed on the track improves, as she puts herself through a strenuous physical training regimen. Throughout the entire preparation for Barcelona, she also has the unwavering support of both of her parents.

Finally, Gail arrives at Barcelona, where her main competition is fellow American Gwen Torrence. On the day of the big race, the television film shows a

Louis Gossett Jr. and Charlayne Woodard portray Bobby Kersee and Gail in Run for the Dream. *The movie brought Gail's struggle with Graves' disease to the attention of millions.*

meeting between Gail and Kersee. As portrayed by Gossett, he is a man not given to sentimental speeches and it is hard for him to express what is in his heart. But he manages to tell her that her life fills him with "awe." And he adds: "Girl, you're a champion."

Gail and Bobby Kersee celebrate her victory in the 100-meter dash at the 1996 Summer Olympics. Kersee was instrumental in her comeback from Graves' disease.

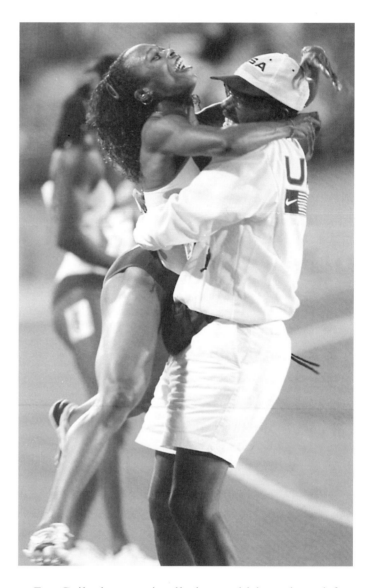

For Gail, the race is all she could have hoped for. She flies down the track and finishes in what looks like a tie with Juliet Cuthbert of Jamaica. Then she has to wait for the judges to review the videotape. As the film shows her, with hands clasped together waiting anxiously for the result, the announcement is finally made

over the loudspeakers at the Olympic stadium: Gail
Devers is the winner.

In the final emotional scenes of the film, Gail looks
for Kersee, who comes toward her through a crowd of
photographers and hugs her. "You got it!" he says.
Then he drapes the American flag around her shoul-
ders. The film reflects the key to Gail's great success—
the combination of a gifted, hard-working athlete and
a world-class coach.

Despite a series of injuries, Gail continues to pursue her dreams of more Olympic gold. She's seen here competing in the women's 60 meters at the 1997 World Indoor Athletics Championship.

7

GAIL KEEPS
ON RUNNING

AFTER THE 1996 Olympics Gail didn't cut back on her racing schedule at all. At the Mobil Invitational Championships in February 1997, Gail bested Gwen Torrence in the 60-meter dash with a time of 7.07 seconds, .05 seconds ahead of Torrence. A week later, Gail beat Torrence again—this time at the United States Indoor Track and Field Championships. Her time was an incredible 7.00 seconds. Although she was recovering from a torn muscle in her leg, she helped the U.S. team win a gold medal in the 4 x 100 relay race at the World Outdoor Championships later that year. In recognition of her accomplishments, Gail, along with soccer star Mia Hamm, was voted the Women's Sports Foundation's 1997 Sportswomen of the Year.

During 1998 injuries prevented Gail from competing in the hurdle events. In 1999 she seemed to be suffering again from problems with her hamstring, and she had trouble with her medication for Graves' disease. In the spring, she finished fifth in a 100-meter hurdle race. But at the World Track and Field Championships in Seville, Spain, Gail returned to form. She set a U.S. record in the hurdles with a time of 12.37 seconds.

While Gail was happy with her performance, she was quick to add, "It's not about accolades or what other people think about me. It's what I think about myself. It was like that even coming back from Graves' disease." She has always seemed self-contained with a strong center, a well-focused inner self. This has continued to help her keep an eye on the most important goals.

Also competing in the hurdles at Seville was Swedish star Ludmila Engquist, who finished third. Engquist, who was in a much tougher battle against cancer, had lost her right breast to surgery in April and had started chemotherapy. "I was proud of her, that she came back and accomplished what she did," Gail said after hugging Engquist when she finished the race. "It lets everybody know if you believe in yourself, dreams do come true."

Gail might have been referring to herself. The Graves' disease that she had been battling since 1988 seemed to trouble her again in 1999. Gail said she had some difficulty eating and sleeping, and her body was aching. Nevertheless, her time was the best since Engquist set the record in 1992. However, Gail admitted she had a tense moment as she crossed the last hurdle in the race. "I was trying to attack the hurdles and I didn't want 1992 to come back at me," she said.

As 2000 began, Gail seemed to have a good chance to win gold once again, at the Olympics in Sydney, Australia. In July, she won the 100-meter hurdles at the Athletissima Tournament in Lausanne, Switzerland, with a time of 12.50 seconds. Earlier she had finished second in the 100-meter dash and the 100-meter hurdles at the IAAF Grand Prix track meet in Croatia.

Approaching the Summer Olympics in September, Gail seemed to be the woman to beat in the 100-meter hurdles. She had already set an American record in the U.S. Olympic trials with a time of 12.33 seconds. But in the semifinal qualifying round at the Olympics in Sydney, the unexpected happened. Although leading as she leapt over the fourth hurdle, Gail stopped suddenly before reaching the fifth. She had torn her hamstring. It seemed as if bad luck had stricken her once again. But Gail, who is not a person to make excuses, saw it differently. "I don't think luck has anything to do with track and field," she said. "I think it's skill. I'd say my skills were not good enough to keep me going tonight. And that's the end of the story."

Gail shares a light moment with tennis legend Billie Jean King and race car driver Lyn St. James (right). They were attending the 1999 Women's Sports Foundation's 20th Annual Salute to Women in Sports, at which Gail was named "Sportswoman of the Year."

Gail pulled up before the fifth hurdle after tearing a hamstring in the qualifying round of the 100-meter hurdles at the 2000 Summer Olympics. She insisted that her Olympic career would continue, however.

But it wasn't entirely over. As Gail put it, "[T]his does not mean that Gail Devers's Olympic dream is over. It just means it wasn't in God's plans today. There are other Olympics." And Gail is expected to compete in them.

There's more to Gail Devers than being a track star. She has committed time and money to helping others with thyroid problems, and the Gail Devers Foundation looks to help youngsters fulfill their potential.

8

BEYOND OLYMPIC GOLD

ALTHOUGH TRACK IS a central part of Gail Devers's life, there arc other things beyond Olympic racing that are very important to her. When she was still a little girl, Gail wanted to become an elementary school teacher, following the role model presented by her mother. As she grew older, Gail held on to her career goal of working with children. But she decided that to really help them, it was necessary to intervene in their lives before elementary school. Her current plan is to open a day care center after she finishes her career in competitive track.

Meanwhile, Gail has found other ways of giving back to society some of the fruits of her own success. "When I look at what I've accomplished during my life thus far," she explains, "I realize I've been truly blessed. Now I want to share my good fortune by passing it on and helping others. Then, I'll consider myself a true champion."

In 1998 Gail received the President's Achievement Award from the American Medical Women's Association for her commitment to Your Thyroid: Gland Central. This program operates across the country, bringing the message of thyroid disease awareness to thousands of people. Started in 1996, Gland Central has already screened almost 10,000 people who may be at risk for thyroid disease, the illness that struck Gail Devers in 1988. Screenings have already occurred in 32 American cities. In addition, Gland Central has committed itself to promote thyroid education in communities throughout the country. As Gail put it: "Thyroid disease could have cost me my dreams if I had let it go undetected any longer." If untreated, the disease can dangerously increase cholesterol levels and damage internal organs, as well as leading to infertility among women. Women are far more susceptible than men to contracting thyroid disease. Indeed, many women who may be experiencing exhaustion and other symptoms Gail had when she tried out for the Olympics in 1988 could actually be suffering from a thyroid disease.

The American Medical Women's Association sponsors Gland Central. Debra Judelson, MD, past president of the association, explains that "thyroid testing makes sense for the adult population at large, particularly for those who are at high risk such as women and the elderly."

In addition to her work as a spokesperson for Gland Central, Gail Devers also started her own foundation in 1999. As Gail put it: "Throughout the years, I've encountered many challenges and had to reach inside myself for powerful spiritual and physical forces to make it through. These forces enabled me to become successful. Now it's time for me to give back." The main focus of the Gail Devers Foundation is helping young people realize their potential, regardless of their race, economic circumstances, or background.

One of the major programs of the foundation is raising

money for the Gail Force Enhancement Center. This center will offer educational programs, training in sports, mentoring, and career development for young people so they can have an opportunity to become successful. As Gail explains, the center will "level the playing field by providing all people with access" to the same chance at getting ahead in their lives.

Even before the center is constructed, the foundation is already helping young people in their communities. In 2000, the foundation began to offer scholarships to youth who planned to go to college. Each Christmas, the foundation also organizes a "Holiday of Cheer"

Gail teamed with the American Medical Women's Association in Philadelphia to launch a statewide thyroid disease awareness campaign. Mayor Ed Rendell proclaimed May 4, 1999, "Thyroid Disease Awareness Day."

Gail Devers combines a strong spiritual foundation with a solid work ethic, drive, and determination to be the best she can be.

program, providing needy families with food, clothing, and presents. Corporations who have become sponsors of the foundation include the Atlanta Braves, Courtyard Marriott, Home Depot, and Target stores. On the foundation website, *www.gaildevers.com,* individuals can learn about joining Club Force, which supports the foundation.

The foundation helps to spread Gail Devers's dreams and values. She has combined a strong spiritual foundation with a solid work ethic, drive, and determination to be the best. These values not only propelled Gail to the top of her field, but also sustained her during the tough times when she was stricken with Graves' disease and believed her career as a track star was over. Her courage, belief in God, and confidence in herself brought Gail back and made her even more successful—as an Olympic star and, more important, as a person.

CHRONOLOGY

1966	Yolanda Gail Devers born on November 19 in Seattle, Washington.
1982–4	Wins three state titles, four Southern California regional titles.
1984	Graduates from Sweetwater High School and enters UCLA.
1987	Takes first place in six events in Pacific 10 Championships.
1988	Sets fastest time for an American woman in 100 meters at Pacific Coast Conference Championships. Attends Olympics in Seoul, South Korea, but does poorly.
1988–90	Battles Graves' disease.
1991	Wins 100-meter hurdles at USA/Mobil Championships.
1992	Wins gold medal in 100-meter dash at Olympics in Barcelona, Spain; honored at Sweetwater High School.
1993	Sets new American record in 60-meter dash at USA/Mobil Indoors; voted U.S. Olympic Committee Sportswoman of the Year; wins 100-meter dash at World Track & Field Championships in Stuttgart, Germany.
1994–5	Battles injuries and does not compete in many events.
1995	Wins 100-meter hurdles in Gothenburg, Sweden; ranked #1 in the world.
1996	Wins gold medal in 100-meter dash at Olympics in Atlanta, Georgia.
1997	Voted Women's Sports Foundation's Sportswoman of the Year.
1998–9	Battles injuries that reduce her number of competitions.
1999	Wins 100-meter hurdles at World Track and Field Championships in Seville, Spain.
2000	Competes in Olympics in Sydney, Australia, but hamstring injury forces her out of qualifying race.

BIBLIOGRAPHY

"A couple of really close calls, Gail takes 100 gold in photo finish." *USAToday.com,* August 17, 1993.

American Medical Women's Association. "Olympian Gail Devers Honored at Annual Meeting." [*www.amwa-doc.org/healthtopics/thyroid5.]* November 19, 1998.

Borges, Ron. "Allegations assume center stage; Torrence's gold in 200, Gail's fall in hurdles overshadowed by talk of drugs." *Boston Globe,* August 7, 1992.

Bradley, Mark. "Gail's composure always in style." *Atlanta Journal-Constitution,* August 1, 1996.

Chronicle of the Olympics, 1896–1996. New York: ADK Publishing, 1996.

CNNSI.com. "Torn dream." September 27, 2000.

Cobbs, Chris. "Running or Jumping, Gail a Hit at 100, Her Goal Is Gold." *Los Angeles Times,* May 15, 1987.

Concannon, Joe. "Gail outraces ordeals." *Boston Globe,* June 15, 1996.

_____. "Gail dashes to world win in women's 60." *Boston Globe,* March 13, 1993.

Cool running. "The Top Runners of the 20th Century: Women." *www.coolrunning.com/20century/20th13w.*

Downey, Mike. "Atlanta 1996 Olympics." *Los Angeles Times,* July 28, 1996.

_____. "U.S. Sprinter Outruns Fear to Win Gold." *Los Angeles Times,* August 2, 1992.

Dyer, Nicole. "Born to Run," *Science World,* September 4, 2000.

Fish, Mike. "Gail Devers 'I just needed to run,' For Gail, one hurdle remains." *Atlanta Journal-Constitution,* July 29, 1996.

Florence, Mal. "Gail Does Her Part as UCLA Sweeps USC in Coliseum Track Meet." *Los Angeles Times,* May 1, 1988.

Gail Devers Foundation. *www.gailGail.com/gailGailfoundation*

Garcia, Irene. "Bruin Gail Devers Steps into Spotlight." *Los Angeles Times,* May 28, 1987.

Grace & Glory: A Century of Women in the Olympics. Chicago: Triumph Books, 1996.

BIBLIOGRAPHY

"Graves' Disease."
www.thyroid.org/patient/brochur3

Gutman, Bill. *Overcoming the Odds: Gail Devers.* Austin, Tex.: Raintree Steck-Vaughn, 1996.

Hersh, Philip. "Gail Devers finally takes spotlight, winning 100-meter hurdles." *Chicago Tribune,* August 28, 1999.

Jackson, Colin. *The Young Track and Field Athlete.* New York: ADK Publishing, 1996.

Jacobson, Steve. "A Real Comeback After 2 1/2 Years, UCLA's Gail Devers Gets Graves Disease Under Control." *Los Angeles Times,* January 30, 1992.

Joyner-Kersee. *A Kind of Grace.* New York: Warner Books, 1997.

Kaminsky, Marty. "A Sprinter's Close Call." *Highlights for Children,* May 1998.

Lee, John. "Conquering Hero Olympic Champion Gail Devers Makes Her Triumphant Return to National City." *Los Angeles Times,* October 20, 1992.

Lindgren, Jim. "Sweetwater Honors Fulfillment of a Dream." *Los Angeles Times,* October 9, 1992.

Mead, Katherine. *Gail Devers, A Runner's Dream.* Austin, Tex.: Raintree Steck-Vaughn, 1998.

Moore, Kenny. "Gail Force." *Sports Illustrated,* May 10, 1993.

Patrick, Dick. "Romance takes on golden glow; Gail, Harrison share title moments." *USAToday.com,* July 28, 1996.

_____. "Torrence wins gold, revives drug charges." *USAToday.com,* August 7, 1992.

_____. "Gail never gave up her dream." *USAToday.com,* August 3, 1992.

Rosenthal, Bert. "Gail wins 100 hurdles, Engquist takes third." *The Oregonian,* August 29, 1999.

Senn, Alfred. *Power, Politics, and the Olympic Games.* Champaign, Ill.: Human Kinetics, 1999.

Warner, Rick. "Gail Loses, Bubka Drops Out, O'Brien Goes for Gold." *www.newstimes.com/archive,* August 1, 1996.

Zeigler, Mark. "Gail hamstrung again on hurdles."
www.signonsandiego.com

WEBSITES

American Association of Clinical Endocrinologists (AACE)
http://www.aace.com/serv/searchindex.htm
Enter your city and state to find an endocrinologist in your area.

The American Foundation of Thyroid Patients
http://thyroid.about.com/library/weekly/aa112497.htm
A look at this growing, patient-founded and patient-oriented foundation and how you can get involved.

American Thyroid Association
http://www.thyroid.org
The official website of the American Thyroid Association has undergone major improvements in design and many content updates. The newly improved site helps with research and finding patient information.

HealthTOUCH
http://www.healthtouch.com/bin/EContent_HT/SUB_HD.asp?goto_type=
1x5-Grid&index=119038&title=Thyroid+Problems&cid=HT
Get information on thyroid problems from HealthTOUCH.

National Graves' Disease Foundation
http://www.ngdf.org/
The site offers information about the National Graves' Disease Foundation and Graves' disease.

Support
http://thyroid.about.com/cs/orgssupport/index.htm
Support groups, thyroid patient organizations, and thyroid-related professional organizations, offering information and/or support for people with thyroid disease, including hypothyroidism, hyperthyroidism, and thyroid cancer.

Thyroid Disease Manager
http://www.thyroidmanager.org/
This site offers an up-to-date analysis of thyrotoxicosis, hypothyroidism, thyroid nodules and cancer, thyroiditis, and all aspects of human thyroid disease and thyroid physiology.

Thyroid Federation International Home Page
http://www.thyroid-fed.org/
Through this site you can stay informed of the activities of this growing organization and the development of existing and future thyroid member organizations in the world.

Thyroid Operation
http://www.endocrineweb.com/surthroid.html
This site analyzes several surgical options for the thyroid gland depending on the problem.

Thyroid Society
http://www.the-thyroid-society.org/
There are more than 20 million Americans with thyroid disease and most of those do not know they have the disease.

APPENDIX

Famous People with Thyroid Conditions

Kim Alexis (model)

Barbara Bush (former first lady)

George Bush (former president)

Gail Devers (track star)

Tipper Gore (wife of former vice president Al Gore)

Bobby Labonte (race car driver)

Carl Lewis (track star)

Carla Overbeck (soccer player)

Joe Piscopo (comedian)

Rod Stewart (rock star)

INDEX

INDEX

INDEX

PICTURE CREDITS

Page

2: Eric Feferberg/Agence France Presse

10: Eric Risberg/AP/Wide World Photos

13: Diether Endlicher/AP/Wide World Photos

15: Mark Duncan/AP/Wide World Photos

17: Michael Rondo/KRT

18: Dean Rutz/KRT

20: Mike Powell/Allsport Photos

22: New Millennium Images

24: New Millennium Images

25: Eric Risberg/AP/Wide World Photos

26: Mitchell Rebel/Al Photo Service

30: Charles Fox/KRT

33: Tim Chapman/KRT

34: Eric Feferberg/Agence France Presse

36: New Millennium Images

39: AP/Wide World Photos

41: KRT Photos Archive

42: AP/Wide World Photos

45: Fred Chartrand/CP/AP/Wide World Photos

50: AP/Wide World Photos

53: Pascal Pavani/Agence France Presse

56: Gary Bogdon/KRT

59: Frank Kleefeldt/Agence France Presse

61: Panworld Sports/Icon Sport Photos

63: Julian H. Gonzalez/KRT

65: David Bergman/KRT

69: Everett Collection

70: William Snyder/KRT

72: Mark Thompson/Agence France Presse

75: Diane Bondareff/AP/Wide World Photos

76: Olivier Morin/Agence France Presse

78: Nancy Kaszerman/Zuma Press

81: Mark Stehle/AP/Wide World Photos

82: Julio Munoz/EFE Photos

Cover photo: AP/Wide World Photos

Richard Worth has 30 years of experience as a writer, trainer, and video producer. He has written more than 25 books, including *The Four Levers of Corporate Change,* a best-selling business book. Many of his books are for young adults, on topics that include family living, foreign affairs, biography, and history. He has also written an eight-part radio series on New York mayor Fiorello LaGuardia, which aired on National Public Radio. He presents writing and public speaking seminars for corporate executives.

James Scott Brady serves on the board of trustees with the Center to Prevent Handgun Violence and is the vice chairman of the Brain Injury Foundation. Mr. Brady served as assistant to the President and White House press secretary under President Ronald Reagan. He was severely injured in an assassination attempt on the president, but remained the White House press secretary until the end of the administration. Since leaving the White House, Mr. Brady has lobbied for stronger gun laws. In November 1993, President Bill Clinton signed the Brady Bill, a national law requiring a waiting period on handgun purchases and a background check on buyers.